The Ultimate Fun in North Carolina

Dog Parks, Hiking Trails, Lodging, Events and More!

By Suzanne Jalot

OLLIEDOG MEDIA, INC. • WILMINGTON, NC

The Ultimate Guide to Doggy Fun in North Carolina

© 2009 by Suzanne Jalot

ISBN:978-0-9843405-0-7

Published by
OllieDog Media, Inc.
PO Box 1914
Wilmington, NC 28402

Printed in the U.S.A.
First edition, 2009

All photos by author unless otherwise noted.

To Ollie and August, who always know how to have a good doggy day; to Ryan, for his encouragement and support; and to my parents, who never stopped believing in the things I could accomplish.

Table of Contents

Introduction

How empty would our lives be without our dogs? Ever since adopting my dog Ollie in 2000, I've been on the hunt for activities that we can both be involved in. Through the years we've gone on many adventures together and explored new places in North Carolina and beyond.

For those fellow dog-lovers, who wouldn't imagine leaving your best friend at home, this book is for you.

The guide is divided into three sections of the state: Mountains, Piedmont and Coast. I couldn't possibly include all the great places to take your dog in North Carolina, but I tried to touch on the highlights of different areas across the state.

I hope you and your furry traveling companion find this book helpful and make your own memories exploring the state. If you have suggestions on fun dog outings or a favorite trail for the next edition of this guide, please let me know!

Author Suzanne Jalot with her traveling companions, Ollie and August

How to use this guide

The guide is divided into three regions: Mountains, Piedmont and Coast. Within each region you'll find cities grouped by area. Under each city you'll find accommodations, dining, dog parks and trails of special interest.

At the end of each region is a list of state parks within the region, a listing of dog parks by city, regional events and emergency vets.

Wherever you see a "FUN STUFF" you'll read about other noteworthy things to do with your pooch.

A note about dining...

Officially, North Carolina health department rules do not allow dogs in restaurants. As of press time, there is also some controversy over whether they are allowed in outdoor seating areas. Any restaurants we have listed are simply known to have hosted canines at outdoor tables in the past. It is up to you to check with the restaurant in advance to see if your pet is welcome.

A note about accommodations...

Accommodations in this book were chosen based on pet-friendliness and user reviews. There may be other places that will accommodate pets, but I looked for places that have the fewest restrictions. It is my opinion that a hotel that will only accept pets under 15 pounds or that restricts breeds is not pet-friendly.

Policies may change so please check with the hotel directly before making any plans. Please also note that a facility's inclusion in this book does not imply an endorsement by the publisher or author.

Etiquette—Such a simple concept, but so often overlooked by many dog owners. This book is all about going out and about with your dog, so manners are a must in public situations.

Hiking: The do's and don'ts of walking the trail

Do keep your dog on a tight leash.

Don't let your dog wander off the trail and destroy vegetation.

Do pick up after your dog. Always!

Don't hog the trail. Allow others plenty of room to pass.

Do pay attention to what your dog is doing.

Don't let your dog approach other dogs on the trail until you get the okay from the owner.

Ollie is a seasoned pro on the trail.

Do pull your dog to the side when passing walkers/hikers without dogs. It's the polite thing to do.

Don't be afraid to have fun!

Dining with Fido

It's a refreshing experience to be able to dine outside with your best canine friend at your feet. Due to health regulations, only service dogs are allowed inside restaurants. Outdoor dining is a different story. North Carolina health department rules seem to be open to interpretation when it comes to whether dogs are actually allowed in outdoor seating areas. Even so, there are many restaurants throughout the state who will cater to your furry friend.

A pleasant meal is easily ruined by an unruly canine diner. Be realistic about your dog's ability to be obedient in a dining situation. If you know your dog might be a problem, don't take him with you. There are plenty of other activities you can both be involved in.

- Don't let your dog eat from your plate
- Bring a water bowl and treats for your dog
- Know your dog's limitations, if he can't sit still for thirty minutes or if you know he constantly lunges at strangers, maybe take-out is best
- Always pay attention to what your dog is doing
- Keep your dog on a leash at all times

Event Manners

Across the state, there is no lack of events to which you can take your dog. We should remember that good manners are especially important when there are dogs in every direction. As with any public outing, if your dog doesn't play well with others, make sure he is muzzled and/or on a tight leash at all times.

Speaking of tight leashes, that's pretty good advice for all dog owners at events. I can't stress enough the importance of paying attention to your dog at all times. Don't just let your dog wander in one direction while you're standing at a booth or talking to another dog owner.

And by all means, don't pretend not to notice when your dog uses the sidewalk as a restroom. Please, just pick it up!

The Unwritten Rules of the Dog Park

By J. W. Swink, originally published in Dog Living Magazine

Dog parks are becoming more prevalent across the state, and dog owners are making their local dog park the popular spot in town. While these additions to the community have many benefits, like most new trends, they also require the introduction of new social etiquette. So, for an enjoyable visit for both you and your canine companion, commit to memory the following un-written rules of the dog park:

1. Children should be kept close by or on leash.*
Yes, your two-legged children are welcome along with your four-legged children at the dog park. While this is a great opportunity to teach children proper etiquette around dogs, this does not mean that children are welcome to roam around screaming, off-leash. When your child gets taken down by a racing pack of dogs, guess who is to blame? Hint: It's not the dogs.

2. Leave your designer clothes at home.
While my dogs have been trained not to jump up on humans, they might forget their manners in all of the excitement. So, while I will certainly apologize to you when my dog leaves muddy paw prints all over you white, terry-cloth Juicy Couture track suit, I'll be laughing at you on the inside. Who wears white to a dog park?

3. Hands off other people's dogs.
It is not your job, nor is it your right, to discipline other people's dogs. If a dog jumps up on you, you have the right to say "OFF" and push him down. If a dog is becoming too aggressive, by all means you have the right to intervene. But, and I'm talking to you, crazy lady who dresses your pugs in Care Bear shirts, if I catch you using your squirt-bottle again on my dog while he is playing, I'll come down on you like the wrath of Khan.

4. Pay attention to your own dog.

It is your duty to monitor your own dog's behavior. There is a brief window of time while a foul is being committed for you to come and intervene. If you are too engrossed in your cell phone conversation to help, you will receive the stink-eye while I yank your dog off of mine. If you find that you are often the recipient of the stink-eye, do not visit a dog park again until your dog has graduated cum laude from the Academy of Canine Manners. (And you might want to brush up on your social skills, too.)

Photo by Jacob Rudolph

5. Leave your designer dogs at home, too.

Are you really not into dogs, but bought your cross-bred designer miniature because they have been deemed the latest accessory? Do you like being seen at the dog park but think your dog is too fragile (or too precious) to play with others? Then the dog park is not for you. When you sit on a bench with your dog in your lap, or when you carry your dog in your arms, you have a big, milk-bone flavored sign on your forehead begging all dogs to jump up on you. You have started a game of keep away, and your tiny accessory is 'it'. So, please, go back to parading your four-pound accessory around Harris Teeter or Belk's for your daily dose of attention.

6. Humping is bad form.
Unless you are in middle school, there is nothing really funny about watching a dog hump another dog. Please correct your dog immediately if he can't keep his paws to himself. Your dog will gain the reputation of a chronic humper with an inferiority complex and will soon find himself without any furry playmates. Nobody likes a bully, and we don't care for their enabling owners, either.

7. The dog park is not your private backyard.
Remember that dog parks are public spaces. I understand that your four-by-six concrete patio is cramping your style and that your Springer Spaniel is itching to play fetch, but you still have to share the park with other dogs. So don't get upset when you throw your tennis ball across the park and 14 Goldens out-race your dog to retrieve it. And you are even more deluded if you expect to leave with the same ball you brought.

The happiest dogs I have ever seen are ones in dog parks, and if it were up to me all dogs would get this privilege. They get to play, run, jump, chase, wrestle and sniff until they tire their drooling selves out. So, if you haven't treated your most loyal companion to a visit to your local dog park, what are you waiting for? You are now versed on proper dog park etiquette, and that four-by-six concrete patio isn't getting any bigger.

*Some dog parks have posted rules forbidding children under 12 from entering.

The Mountains

The mountains of North Carolina are a hikers paradise. Whether you and your dog are experienced or novice, there's a trail for you. But hiking isn't the only thing to do in the North Carolina mountains.

The city of Asheville is a diverse community with a rich cultural history in the heart of the Blue Ridge and Great Smoky Mountains. It boasts friendly people and an eclectic mix of things to do. It's here you'll find America's largest home, the Biltmore Estate. Asheville has also been voted one of the most dog-friendly cities in North Carolina.

Well to the north of Asheville, Boone is a vibrant town featuring mountain sunsets and true southern hospitality. You can enjoy comfortable temperatures in the summer and white winters. It's also been named one of America's best small towns.

There's no lack of attractions to explore in the surrounding areas either. So head west, where adventures await you and your dog from the Blue Ridge Parkway to Grandfather Mountain.

Asheville and Surrounding Areas

Asheville

Accommodations—Bed & Breakfasts

Black Walnut Bed & Breakfast
800-381-3878
288 Montford Ave, Asheville, NC 28801
www.blackwalnut.com

Carolina Bed & Breakfast
888-254-3608
177 Cumberland Ave, Asheville, NC 28801
www.carolinabb.com

1889 WhiteGate Inn & Cottage
800-485-3045
173 E. Chestnut St, Asheville, NC 28801

1900 Inn on Montford
800-254-9569
296 Montford Ave, Asheville, NC 28801

 # FUN STUFF!

Ghost Hunters of Asheville Tours
Take your dog on a hunt for the supernatural. Several different tours are available and leashed dogs are welcome on all of them.

Most tours leave from the Haywood Park Hotel located at 1 Battery Park Avenue.

For reservations call 282-779-HUNT or go online for more information at www.ghosthuntersofasheville.com.

Accommodations—Hotels/Motels

Crown Plaza Resort Asheville
828-254-3211
One Holiday Inn Dr, Asheville, NC 28806

Days Inn Asheville Mall
828-252-4000
201 Tunnel Rd, Asheville, NC 28805

Downtown Inn & Suites
828-254-9661
120 Patton Ave, Asheville, NC 28801

Ramada Inn Asheville
828-298-9141
800 Fairview Rd, Asheville, NC 28803

Red Roof Inn Asheville West
828-667-9803
16 Crowell Rd, Asheville, NC 28806

FUN STUFF!

The Soapy Dog
Go ahead and get dirty. The Soapy Dog offers do-it-yourself dog washing at 270 Depot Street in Asheville.

Visit them online at www.thesoapydog.com or call 828-350-0333.

Campgrounds

Pisgah National Forest
828-877-3350
1001 Pisgah Hwy, Asheville, NC 28768

 # FUN STUFF!

Four Paws Kingdom

Located in the foothills of the North Carolina mountains in Rutherfordton, Four Paws Kingdom is 32 acres of doggy fun.

The campground includes a fully fenced dog park and agility fun playground, a rally obedience arena, a fully fenced off-leash area with creek access, doggy bathhouse and grooming stations, 20 acres of natural hiking trails, and a doggy swimming pond.

Private obedience, behavior and agility training classes are available along with dog walking services.

If you don't have an RV, not to worry. Four Paws Kingdom has a limited number of RVs for rent, as well as cabins. Check it out at www.4pawskingdom.com.

Dog and Dine

Asheville Pizza and Brewing Company
828-254-5339
675 Merrimon Ave, Asheville, NC 28804
www.ashevillepizza.com

Sunny Point Café & Bakery
828-252-0055
626 Haywood Rd, Asheville, NC 28806
www.sunnypointcafe.com

Posana Cafe
828-505-3969
One Biltmore Ave, Asheville, NC 28801
www.posanacafe.com

Urban Burrito
828-251-1921
640 Merrimon Ave, Asheville, NC 28804
www.urbanburrito.com

Grove Arcade

A collection of shops and dining options await you at the beautifully renovated Grove Arcade. Dogs are not allowed in the building, but are welcome in the market area and the outdoor dining areas of some of the restaurants.

1 Page Avenue, Asheville, NC 28801
828-252-7799/www.grovearcade.com

Dog Parks

Azalea Park
498 Azalea Road
Free

French Broad River Park
180 Amboy Road
Free

Barkwells

Just twenty minutes outside of Asheville, Barkwells is more than eight acres of fenced-in fun for you and your dog. Go ahead and drop the leash! This resort truly understands the bond between dogs and their owners. Humans will enjoy soaking in the hot tub on the deck of their cottage. Later, you can curl up with your furry friend in front of a cozy fireplace.

290 Lance Road, Mills River, NC 28759
828-891-8288
www.barkwells.com

Black Mountain

Accommodations—Hotels/Motels

Super 8
828-669-8076
101 Flat Creek Rd, Black Mountain, NC 28711

 **FUN STUFF!**

Chimney Rock Park
Although this is a state park, it is operated by a private contractor and is known for being super dog-friendly. While the entrance fee may be a little steep at $14, it's well worth a visit. No matter which trails you choose to explore, you and your dog will be delighted.

800-277-9611/www.chimneyrockpark.com

Burnsville
Accommodations—Hotels/Motels
Blue Ridge Motel
828-682-9100
204 West Blvd, Burnsville, NC 28714

Mountain View Motel
828-682-2115
Hwy 19 East, Burnsville, NC 28714

Campgrounds
Mount Mitchell State Park
828-675-4611
2388 Hwy 128, Burnsville, NC 28714

Trails to Sniff Out

The North Carolina Arboretum, Asheville
More than 10 miles of hiking trails from easy to difficult await visitors to this popular destination. Parking will cost you $6.

Getting There: *From I-40 West, merge onto Interstate 26 East. Take Exit 33 and turn left on Hwy 191. Follow brown signs to NC Arboretum.*

Biltmore Estate, Asheville
Pets are not allowed in the buildings, but they are welcome on the grounds of this 125,000 acre estate. Hire a pet-sitter and you can explore the 250-room house sans Fido.

Getting There: *For detailed directions visit www.biltmore.com.*

The Urban Trail, Asheville

Stop by the visitor's center and pick up a map for this nearly two mile, self-guided tour of downtown Asheville. Pink granite markers in the sidewalk blaze this trail along with sculptures and plaques indicating items of historical and architectural significance.

Getting There: *The Urban Trail is located in downtown Asheville and begins at 2 South Pack Square in Pack Place.*

Graveyard Fields, Big East Fork

This well-marked trail is a loop that will take you about two hours. A popular spot on the Blue Ridge Parkway, it can get crowded, so avoid the summer and fall months and plan for an off-season trip. You'll discover waterfalls, boulders, a stream and forest throughout this nearly 3.5 mile trail.

Getting There: *The trail is located off of milepost 418 on the Blue Ridge Parkway.*

Old Mitchell Trail, Burnsville

This trail is not for the meek! Mount Mitchell is the highest peak in the eastern U.S. and hikers will be rewarded with stunning views of the mountains. You can expect to encounter steep, wet rocks, so make sure both you and your dog are up for the challenge of this trail.

Getting There: *From Asheville, take the Blue Ridge Parkway north to milepost 355 and follow signs to Mount Mitchell State Park.*

Fryingpan Mountain Trail, Cruso

This trail is next to the Mount Pisgah Campground and not as widely used as some of the others along the Blue Ridge Parkway. Wildflowers line the trail during the spring, summer and fall and your dog will have plenty to sniff. The trail is about four miles and should take between two and three hours.

Getting There: *The Mount Pisgah Campground is located at milepost 408 on the Blue Ridge Parkway. Turn into the campground and you will see a sign for the trail on the left.*

TRAIL TIP: Know both your limits and your dog's limits, especially on longer hikes. Don't try to do too much in one day. If your dog shows signs of fatigue, don't be afraid to simply sit down and rest for awhile.

Boone and surrounding areas

Banner Elk

Accommodations—Hotels/Motels

Best Western Mountain Lodge
828-898-4571
1615 Tynecastle Hwy 184, Banner Elk, 28604

Shawnee Mountain Lodge
828-963-6200
595 Shawnee Rd, Banner Elk, 28604

Blowing Rock

Accommodations—Hotels/Motels

Blowing Rock Victorian Inn
828-295-0034
242 Ransom St, Blowing Rock, NC 28605
www.blowingrockvictorianinn.com

Dog and Dine

Tijuana Fats
828-295-9683
1182 Main St, Blowing Rock, NC 28692

 FUN STUFF!

The Blowing Rock

North Carolina's oldest travel attraction, no section on the mountains would be complete without a mention of The Blowing Rock.

The cliff is 4,000 feet above sea level and is so named because light objects thrown from the rock will return due to the wind and the unique shape of the rocky walls of the gorge.

This attraction is located near Boone off the Blue Ridge Parkway on highway 321 South and admission is $6 for adults.

828-295-7111
www.theblowingrock.com

Boone

Dog Parks

Watauga Humane Society Dog Park
Don Hayes Road
Application-based with annual fees

 **FUN STUFF!**

Mast General Store

For a step back in time, visit the Mast General Store. The original location dates back to 1883. You'll find one-of-a-kind nostalgic items along with a more modern line of pet products. They also have treats on hand for pets who stop by. Visit online at www.mastgeneralstore.com for a list of locations.

Lenoir

Accommodations—Hotels/Motels

Days Inn
828-754-0731
206 Blowing Rock Blvd, Lenoir, NC 28645

Jameson Inn
828-758-1200
350 Wilkesboro Blvd, Lenoir, NC 28645

 **FUN STUFF!**

Blue Ridge Parkway Auto Tour

Get your dog, back a picnic lunch (and some doggy snacks), grab some road trip tunes and head on out to the Blue Ridge Parkway for a scenic drive. You don't have to drive all 469 miles of this rural parkway, but you can if you want!

The tour follows the Appalachian Mountain chain from Shenandoah National Park to the Great Smoky Mountains National Park.

Along the way there are turnouts where you can view waterfalls, check out visitor centers and stop for a picnic. Note that much of the Parkway is closed in the winter months.

Linville

Accommodations—Bed & Breakfasts

Linville Cottages
877-797-1885
154 Ruffin St, Linville, NC
www.linvillecottages.com

 FUN STUFF!

Grandfather Mountain

In 2008, the North Carolina State Parks system acquired almost 2,500 acres along the crest of Grandfather Mountain, technically making it North Carolina's newest state park. However, the Grandfather Mountain attraction which is located adjacent to the park, still operates as a private entity. You'll find more than 12 miles of hiking trails to explore. Some of the trails should only be attempted by experienced hikers and may not be dog-friendly because of ladders and cables used in the steeper sections. Check with a ranger or staff member for advice.

The Grandfather Mountain attraction is a treat for both you and your pooch. Pets are allowed throughout the park, but not in buildings or in the Animal Habitat areas.

Admission: $15.00 per person
800-468-7325
www.grandfathermountain.com

Trails to Sniff Out

New River State Park, Laurel Springs

Ironically, the New River is thought to be one of the oldest rivers in North America. Several trails are found throughout the park and for the best views of the river, take the Hickory Trail. There are several ways to access the park, but the Visitors Center is located at the US221 access.

Getting There: *Take US 221 through Jefferson and turn onto US221/16N. Go approximately 4.7 miles to Tom Fowler Road and turn right. Go to the stop sign and turn left onto US221 and the park entrance is 2.7 miles on the right.*

Moses H. Cone Memorial Park, Blowing Rock

Dogs aren't allowed in the centerpiece of this park, Cone Manor, but numerous trails and waterways can be found throughout the park's 3600 acres. The park is managed by the National Park Service.

Getting There: *Located at Milepost 295 on the Blue Ridge Parkway, in Blowing Rock.*

Crabtree Falls Loop Trail, Celo

Because of the high elevation and possible closure, this trail is best explored between May and September. Although the trail can get slippery and muddy (sturdy hiking shoes are a must), the payoff is great.

Getting There: *Located at Milepost 339 on the Blue Ridge Parkway at the Crabtree Falls Campground.*

Price Lake Loop Trail, Blowing Rock

As the name suggests, this trail takes you along the shores of beautiful Price Lake and offers opportunities for your pooch to stick his paws in the water for a quick swim. The trail is just over two miles and is a relatively easy hike, over level terrain.

Getting There: *Located near Milepost 297 at the Boone Fork Overlook near Blowing Rock.*

Mount Jefferson State Natural Area, Jefferson

A couple of trails to note:

Summit Trail (0.3 miles): Here you'll ascend to the highest point on Mount Jefferson, although the views here are not the greatest.

Rhododendron Trail (1.1 miles): This trail can be combined with the Summit Trail to form a loop and is a more strenuous hike with better scenery.

Getting There: *From Boone, take US 221 north, cross NC 163 and follow signs to the entrance of the park.*

TRAIL TIP: Trails are exciting places for dogs - so much to sniff and see! Practice with your dog on shorter, less crowded trails if you think your dog might get over-stimulated. And once he gets used to going out on short explorations, he'll be the perfect partner for those long hikes.

State Parks

Gorges State Park
NC 281 South
Sapphire, NC 28774
(828) 966-9099

Hanging Rock State Park
2015 Hanging Rock Park Rd
Danbury, NC 27016
(336) 593-8480

Lake James State Park
2785 Hwy 126
Nebo, NC 28761
(828) 652-5047

Mount Jefferson State Natural Area
S.R. 1152
Jefferson, NC 28640
(336) 246-9653

Mount Mitchell State Park
2388 State Hwy 128
Burnsville, NC 28714
(828) 675-4611

New River State Park
358 US Hwy 221 N Access Rd
Laurel Springs, NC 28644
(336) 982-2587

Pilot Mountain State Park
1792 Pilot Knob Park Rd
Pinnacle, NC 27043
(336) 325-2355

South Mountains State Park
3001 South Mountain Park Ave
Connelly Springs, NC 28612
(828) 433-4772

Stone Mountain State Park
3042 Frank Pkwy
Roaring Gap, NC 28668
(336) 957-8185

Did You Know...

Pets are allowed in all state parks as long as they are on a leash no longer than six feet. When camping, your dog must be kept in your tent or vehicle overnight.

Dogs are not allowed in any building within the state parks, with the exception of service animals.

A ranger could ask you to remove your pet from the park if he is being aggressive or noisy or otherwise disturbing other park guests.

You must pick up after your pet at all times.

Off Leash Dog Parks (by city)

Asheville
Azalea Park
498 Azalea Road
Free

French Broad River Park
180 Amboy Road
Free

Boone
Watauga Humane Society Dog Park
Don Hayes Road
Application-based with annual fees

Events

APRIL   **Bark in the Park,** Chimney Rock Park
               www.chimneyrockpark.com

JULY   **BJ's Dog Show,** Beech Mountain
               www.beechmountainchamber.com
               Coon Dog Day, Saluda
               www.saluda.com

SEPTEMBER   **Blowing Rock Pet Show,** Blowing Rock
               www.wataugahumanesociety.org

OCTOBER   **Watauga Humane Society Dog Jog,** Boone
               www.wataugahumanesociety.org

Emergency Vets

ASHEVILLE   R.E.A.C.H. of Asheville
                       677 Brevard Road
                       Asheville, NC 28806
                       828-665-4399

BOONE   Animal Emergency Clinic
                       1126 Blowing Rock Rd, Ste A
                       Boone, NC 28607
                       828-268-2833

The Piedmont

You'll find plenty for you and your dog to explore in the central portion of the state. Charlotte, the "Queen City" offers a big city feel and a vibrant nightlife. And with a visit to the city you'll quickly discover why Charlotte was named the best walking city in North Carolina by Prevention Magazine.

The triad region includes the three cities of Greensboro, Winston Salem and High Point which are rich in history and home to beautiful natural areas. From Old Salem to downtown Greensboro, there are plenty of places for dogs and humans to explore in the triad.

The capital city of Raleigh is often ranked one of the best places to live in the country offering the attractions of big city life, but at a bit of a slower pace. There are over 150 parks, gardens and lakes in Raleigh and the city boasts one of the most extensive greenway systems in the state.

The Piedmont area is also home to many human-only experiences, so don't be afraid to hire a pet-sitter or drop off your dog at one of the many daycare facilities available and explore on your own for a few hours.

Charlotte and surrounding areas

Charlotte

Accommodations—Hotels/Motels

Comfort Inn Executive Park
704-525-2626
5822 Westpark Dr, Charlotte, NC 28217

Country Hearth Inn Charlotte
704-596-9390
5301 Equipment Drive, Charlotte, NC 28213

Days Inn Charlotte Woodlawn
704-525-5500
118 East Woodlawn Rd, Charlotte, NC 28217

PIEDMONT - Charlotte

Doubletree Guest Suites Charlotte
704-364-2400
6300 Morrison Blvd, Charlotte, NC 28211

Drury Inn & Suites Charlotte North
704-593-0700
415 West T Harris Blvd, Charlotte, NC 28262

 # FUN STUFF!

Charlotte Knights Dog Day
In the mood for a little baseball action? If you're in Charlotte in the spring, check the schedule for "Dog Day" at the park. Baseball fans can enjoy America's favorite pastime with their favorite four-legged pal.

www.minorleaguebaseball.com

Dog and Dine

The Dog Bar
704-370-3595
3307 North Davidson St, Charlotte, NC 28205
www.thedogbar.com

Angry Ale's
704-525-FOOD
1518 Montford Dr, Charlotte, NC 28209
www.angryales.com

Village Bistro
704-369-5190
14815 John J Delaney Dr, Charlotte, NC 28277

FUN STUFF!

The Dog Bar
Located in the NoDa Arts District, this little bar is the perfect spot to grab a drink with your best friend.

There's no discrimination here - Well-behaved dogs of all sizes are welcome to hang out with you while you enjoy a beer or a glass of wine.

There is a membership fee of $10 per dog, but you can get one on your first visit. Vaccination records are required for membership.

Dog Parks

Barkingham Park (at Reedy Creek Park)
2900 Rocky River Road
Free

Davie Dog Park
4635 Pineville-Matthews Road
Free

Frazier Neighborhood Dog Park
1200 West 4th St Ext
Free

Ray's Fetching Meadow (at McAlpine Creek Park)
8711 Monroe Road
Free

Trails to Sniff Out

Latta Park, Charlotte
Cozy would be the word to describe this small, inner city park. It offers wide gravel trails, mature oaks and a creek that runs the entire length of the park.

Getting There: *Latta Park is located at 601 East Park Avenue in Charlotte.*

Crowders Mountain State Park, Kings Mountain
Situated just outside of Charlotte, this state park offers some amazing trails and stunning views that stretch more than 25 miles from the top of the mountain.

Backside Trail (.9 miles): This trail is a lot of work, but well worth it as you end up at the summit of Crowders Mountain.

Fern Trail (1 mile loop): This is a relaxing walk that follows a creek on some portions.

Getting There: *From I-85 South, take Exit 13 and turn left onto Edgewood Road. Turn right at the first stoplight onto Franklin Blvd/Hwy 74. Take a left onto Sparrow Springs Road at the next stoplight. The main entrance will be less than a mile on the right.*

Upper Little Sugar Creek Greenway, Charlotte

This part of the greenway is about a mile long and joins Cordelia Park and Alexander Park.

Getting There: *Access to Little Sugar Creek Greenway is located at the corner of Davidson Street and Parkwood Avenue in Charlotte.*

Morrow Mountain State Park, Albemarle

As with most of the state parks, Morrow Mountain offers a short, easy nature trail as well as extensive hikes. In all, 15 miles of trails are at your disposal. All the trails are clearly marked and one of the best is the hike up to the top of Morrow Mountain, which is a little over 5 miles roundtrip. For a more strenuous hike, however, take the Sugarloaf or Hattaway Mountain trails.

Getting There: *From I-40, take US 220 South and turn right on NC 24, traveling west toward Albemarle. Turn right on Valley Drive and go approximately 3 miles. The entrance to the park will be on your right.*

The Triad and surrounding areas

Greensboro

Accommodations—Hotels/Motels

Red Roof Inn Greensboro Coliseum
336-852-6560
2101 West Meadowview Rd, Greensboro, NC 27403

Baymont Inn & Suites
336-294-6220
2001 Veasley St, Greensboro, NC 27407

Dog and Dine

Fishbones
336-370-4900
2119 Walker Ave, Greensboro, NC 27403

Natty Greene's
336-274-1373
345 South Elm St, Greensboro, NC 27401

 # FUN STUFF!

Mendenhall Plantation
This early 1800's plantation features the main house and several other buildings. Leashed dogs are welcome on the grounds, but not in any of the buildings.

336-454-3819/www.mendenhallplantation.org

Dog Parks

Stephen M. Hussey BarkPark at Country Park
3905 Nathanael Green Drive
Free
www.gsobarkpark.org

 # FUN STUFF!

RagApple Lassie Vineyards
Tastings and tours await, although dogs are not allowed in the buildings, they are welcome on the grounds.

866-RAG-APPLE/www.ragapplelassie.com

Elon

Dog Parks

Elon Dog Park
434 Cook Road
Annual Fee

Trails to Sniff Out

Greensboro Watershed Trails
Not your typical walk in the park, these trails surround Greensboro's municipal reservoirs. There are more than 40 miles of trails to explore.

Getting There: *Located around the city, detailed maps can be found at www.greensboro-nc.gov or by calling 336-373-3816.*

TRAIL TIP: When approaching fellow walkers/hikers without dogs, always yield and give them the right-of-way.

Bethabara Park

This is the site of a 1753 Moravian religious center and trading post. Nature trails are located throughout the park.

Getting There: *Located at 2147 Bethabara Road in Winston Salem.*

The Triangle and surrounding areas

Cary

Accommodations—Hotels/Motels

Comfort Suites
919-852-4318
350 Asheville Ave, Cary, NC 27518

Extended Stay America Cary Regency Parkway
919-468-5828
1701 Regency Pkwy, Cary, NC 27511

Residence Inn by Marriott
919-467-4080
2900 Regency Pkwy, Cary, NC 27518

Towneplace Suites by Marriott
919-678-0005
120 Sage Commons Way, Cary, NC 27513

Dog and Dine

Hibernian Pub
919-467-9000
1144 Kildaire Farm Rd, Cary, NC 27511

 # FUN STUFF!

Jordan Lake Pontoon Tours
Book a private tour with your pooch and his doggy friends for a day on the lake, a sunset cruise, a moonlight tour or even a wine tasting.

The pontoon boat seats up to 13 people and public tours are also available, although bringing your dog isn't an option on those.

Learn more at www.jordanlaketours.com.

Dog Parks

Town of Cary Dog Park (at Godbold Park)
2050 Northwest Maynard Road
Annual memberships and day passes available

Chapel Hill

Dog and Dine

Brixx
919-929-1942
501 Meadowmont Village Circle, Chapel Hill, NC 27517

Dog Parks

The Chapel Hill Dog Park (at Homestead Park)
104 Homestead Road

 FUN STUFF!

North Carolina Botanical Garden
You and your dog can explore nature trails and garden displays at the
North Carolina Botanical Garden.

A pet tie-up post is available for those wanting to explore the fenced-in
areas where dogs are not allowed.

Learn more at www.ncbg.unc.edu.

Durham

Accommodations—Hotels/Motels

America's Best Value Inn Duke
919-286-0771
2517 Guess Rd, Durham, NC 27705

Holiday Inn Express
919-313-3244
2516 Guess Rd, Durham, NC 27705

Sleep Inn Durham
919-993-3393
5208 New Page Rd, Durham, NC 27709

Dog and Dine

Hammock's Cafe
919-293-1050
2121 TW Alexander Dr, Durham, NC 27560

Dog Parks

Durham Dog Park (at Piney Wood Park)
5999 Woodlake Drive
$12/year (residents)/$20/year (non-residents)

Northgate Dog Park
400 W. Lavender Avenue
$12/year (residents)/$20/year (non-residents)

Fayetteville

Dog Parks

Riverside Dog Park
Eastern Boulevard
Free

 FUN STUFF!

Carolina DockDogs
You've seen it on ESPN and the Outdoor Channel, but did you know
North Carolina has it's own chapter of this popular sport?

Events are held throughout the state and if your dog loves the water,
check out one of their open practices! The "home" dock is located at
Old Gilliam Mill Park in Sanford. All breeds are welcome.

For more details and a schedule of events, visit
www.carolinadockdogs.com.

Raleigh

Accommodations—Hotels/Motels

Holiday Inn Raleigh North
919-872-3500
2805 Highwoods Blvd, Raleigh, NC 27604

Fairfield Inn & Suites by Marriott Raleigh Crabtree
919-881-9800
2201 Summit Park Lane, Raleigh, NC 27612

Residence Inn by Marriott Raleigh Midtown
919-878-6100
1000 Navaho Dr, Raleigh, NC 27609

Dog and Dine

101 Lounge & Cafe
919-833-8008
444 S. Blount St, 101 Palladium Plaza, Raleigh, NC 27601
www.101raleigh.com

Lilly's Pizza
919-833-0226
1813 Glenwood Ave, Raleigh, NC 27608
www.lillyspizza.com

Village Draft House
919-833-1373
428 Daniels St, Raleigh, NC 27605

🐾 FUN STUFF!

Raleigh Flea Market
Hundreds of vendors flock to the State Fairgrounds each weekend selling their wares so treasure hunting is ripe. One note: Ignore the peddlers selling puppies and opt to visit the local animal shelter instead. The fairgrounds are located at 1025 Blue Ridge Road in Raleigh.

Dog Parks

Millbrook Exchange Dog Park
1905 Spring Forest Road
Free

Carolina Pines Community Dog Park
2305 Lake Wheeler Road
Free

Oakwood Dog Park
910 Brookside Drive
Free

Wake Forest

Dog Parks

Flaherty Dog Park
1226 N. White Street
Free

Trails to Sniff Out

Johnston Mill Nature Preserve, Chapel Hill

This tract of land is owned by the Triangle Land Conservancy. A one-mile loop trail and a slightly longer one-way trail are located on the preserve. Mature hardwoods and a gently flowing creek await you and your canine pal for this beautiful walk in the woods.

Getting There: *From I-40, take Exit 266. Follow NC 86 North for 1.8 miles. Turn right on Mt. Sinai Road. Go 1.1 miles and the parking lot is on the right, just before the New Hope Creek Bridge.*

William B. Umstead State Park, Raleigh

Twenty miles of hiking trails at this park make you forget you're in the middle of an urban area. There are short, paved trails and longer, more strenuous trails. Some of the trails are not clearly marked, so make sure you stop by the park office and pick up a map before heading out on your hike.

Getting There: *From I-40, turn northeast on I-540 and take the US 70 exit toward Raleigh. Watch for signs and the park entrance will be on your right.*

Downtown Durham Walking Tour, Durham

This two-mile self-guided tour starts at the Visitors Center and takes you by the historic Durham Athletic Park (Remember the movie *Bull Durham?*), the BC Headache Powder Factory, Durham Central Park, Duke University and many other interesting locations.

Getting There: *Pick up your map at the Durham Convention and Visitors Bureau located at 101 East Morgan Street.*

TRAIL TIP: Always carry bags for picking up after your dog on the trail. Wild animals may be allowed to poop in the woods, but that doesn't mean it's okay for your dog to do it.

Eno River State Park, Durham

This park is huge and boasts over a dozen scenic trails. Here are a few of the best:

Buckquarter Creek (1.5 mile loop): A rock outcropping on this trail gives you a view of the best rapids on the river. It's a bit rocky, so watch out for your four-legged friend.

Cox Mountain (3.75 miles): Hikers get to cross an incredible suspension bridge on this trail. The trail can get steep and goes up to 270 feet in elevation.

Bobbitt Hole (1.65 mile loop): This is one of the most scenic trails in the park showcasing waterfalls and several rock outcroppings.

Dunnagan (1.8 mile loop): Hikers can access this trail via the Pea Creek Trail by crossing the creek on a footbridge. This trail takes you past a cemetery, two old home sites and the remnants of an old dam.

Getting There: *From Interstate 85, take exit 173 and turn onto Cole Mill Rd (heading away from Durham). The park is located at 6101 Cole Mill Road.*

Hemlock Bluffs Nature Preserve, Cary

You'll find nearly three miles of wooded hiking trails and a native wildflower garden to explore at this natural area in Cary. Swift Creek winds through the preserve and it's also a popular spot for bird watchers.

Getting There: *Take I-40 to US1 South. Exit onto Tryon Road and turn right at the third light onto Kildaire Farm Road. The nature preserve will be about a mile and a half on your right.*

Cape Fear River Trail, Fayetteville

Designated as part of the East Coast Greenway, this trail will eventually connect from Maine to Key West! This paved path is just over four miles, one-way and includes wooden bridges, a covered bridge and slightly hilly terrain.

Getting There: *From I-95, take Exit 52 to NC 24 West. Go 4 miles and turn right on US401 Business North (Ramsey Street). Turn right onto Sherman Drive. Park at J. Bayard Clark Park.*

State Parks

Crowders Mountain State Park
522 Park Office Lane
Kings Mountain, NC 28086
(704) 853-5375

Eno River State Park
6101 Cole Mill Road
Durham, NC 27705-9275
(919) 383-1686

Falls Lake State Recreation Area
13304 Creedmoor Rd
Wake Forest, NC 27587
(919) 676-1027

Jordan Lake State Recreation Area
280 State Park Rd
Apex, NC 27523
(919) 362-0586

Kerr Lake State Recreation Area
6254 Satterwhite Point Rd
Henderson, NC 27537
(252) 438-7791

Lake Norman State Park
159 Inland Sea Lane
Troutman, NC 28166
(704) 528-6350

Medoc Mountain State Park
1541 Medoc State Park Rd
Hollister, NC 27844
(252) 586-6588

Morrow Mountain State Park
49104 Morrow Mountain Rd
Albemarle, NC 28001
(704) 982-4402

Raven Rock State Park
3009 Raven Rock Rd
Lillington, NC 27546
(910) 893-4888

Weymouth Woods-Sandhills Nature Preserve
1024 Ft. Bragg Rd
Southern Pines, NC 28387
(910) 692-2167

William B. Umstead State Park
8801 Glenwood Ave
Raleigh, NC 27617
(919) 571-4170

There are 40 state parks
in North Carolina
and over half of them
offer 5 or more miles of
hiking trails

Visit the North Carolina State Park System online at
www.ncparks.gov

Off Leash Dog Parks (by city)

Carrboro
Anderson Community Park

Cary
Town of Cary Dog Park (at Godbold Park)
2050 Northwest Maynard Road
Annual memberships and day passes available

Chapel Hill
The Chapel Hill Dog Park (at Homestead Park)
104 Homestead Road

Charlotte
Barkingham Park (at Reedy Creek Park)
2900 Rocky River Road
Free

Davie Dog Park
4635 Pineville-Matthews Road
Free

Frazier Neighborhood Dog Park
Free

Ray's Fetching Meadow (at McAlpine Creek Park)
8711 Monroe Road
Free

Cornelius
Swaney Pointe K-9 Park (at Ramsey Creek Park)
18441 Nantz Road
Free

Durham
Durham Dog Park (at Piney Wood Park)
5999 Woodlake Drive
$12/year (residents)/$20/year (non-residents)

Northgate Dog Park
400 W. Lavender Avenue
$12/year (residents)/$20/year (non-residents)

Make sure you brush up on dog park etiquette before
hitting the off-leash parks.

Elon
Elon Dog Park
434 Cook Road
Annual Fee

Fayetteville
Riverside Dog Park
Eastern Boulevard
Free

Gastonia
George Poston Dog Park
1101 Lowell Spencer Mountain Road

Greensboro
Stephen M. Hussey BarkPark at Country Park
3905 Nathanael Green Drive
Free
www.gsobarkpark.org

Raleigh
Carolina Pines Community Dog Park
2305 Lake Wheeler Road
Free

Millbrook Exchange Dog Park
1905 Spring Forest Road
Free

Oakwood Dog Park
910 Brookside Drive
Free

Wake Forest
Flaherty Dog Park
1226 N. White Street
Free

What if another dog is bullying my dog at the dog park?

You shouldn't make it a practice to discipline another person's dog at the dog park, but if a dog is being inappropriate, you have every right to interject. If a dog is being too aggressive, do what you can to remove your dog from the situation. However, if another dog is simply stealing your tennis balls, well, maybe you should check back to page 11 of this book to review your dog park etiquette.

Events

MARCH   **Doggie Easter Egg Hunt,** Triangle Area
www.animall.org
Lance Memorial Canines for the Cure NADAC
Agiity Trial, Chapel Hill

APRIL   **Bark Around the Park,** Raleigh
www.raleighnc.gov
SPCA of Wake County K9-3K, Raleigh
www.spcawake.org

MAY   **APS of Durham Walk for the Animals,** Durham
www.apsofdurham.org
Burrito Bash, Pittsboro
www.chathamanimalrescue.org
Petpalooza, Charlotte
www.humanesocietyofcharlotte.org

SEPTEMBER   **Woof-A-Palooza,** Pittsboro
www.chathamanimalrescue.org

OCTOBER   **Dogtoberfest,** New Hill
www.pawfectmatch.org
Paws for Life 5K9 Road Race, Wake Forest
www.fchsnc.org

NOVEMBER   **Mutt Strutt,** Raleigh
www.wakegov.com

Well-behaved dogs and their humans enjoy the Walk for the Animals each year held on the campus of Duke University. Proceeds from the walk benefit the Animal Protection Society of Durham.

Emergency Vets

BURLINGTON

Alamance Animal Emergency Hospital
2643 Ramada Rd
Burlington, NC 27215
336-792-2206

CARY

Animal Emergency Clinic
220 High House Rd
Cary, NC 27513
919-462-8989

CHARLOTTE

Animal Emergency
2225 Township Rd
Charlotte, NC 28273
704-588-7015

GREENSBORO

After Hours Veterinary Clinic
5505 W Friendly Ave
Greensboro, NC 27410
336-851-1990

KANNAPOLIS

Cabarrus Emergency Vet Clinic
1317 S Cannon Blvd
Kannapolis, NC 28083
704-932-1182

RALEIGH

After Hours Animal Emergency
409 Vick Ave
Raleigh, NC
919-781-5145

Not sure if your dog needs emergency care?

If your dog is seriously injured, it's an easy decision to take him to the nearest veterinary clinic. But what about other scenarios? Trouble breathing, bleeding, seizures, difficulty walking, snake bites, eye injuries and difficulty urinating are all cases which need to be evaluated by a veterinarian.

If you're unsure, the best thing to do is call your own vet or the nearest emergency clinic, and tell the doctor your concerns. He or she can then advise if your dog needs to see a vet.

The Coast

Everybody loves the beach and North Carolina has miles of coastline to enjoy. Visitors looking for a remote getaway can head to the Outer Banks where they'll enjoy wide beaches and a laid-back atmosphere.

New Bern is the second oldest town in North Carolina and the birthplace of Pepsi Cola. Situated where the Trent and Neuse Rivers meet, it's an ideal spot for boating dogs. History buffs can explore over 150 historic landmarks, including Tryon Palace (humans only) and you can take Fido out to Croatan National Forest for a good hike.

The charm of downtown Wilmington can't be ignored and the city is also host to plenty of dog events throughout the year. Your dog will love the freedom of romping along the ocean at Freeman Park, in Carolina Beach.

To the south, Brunswick County beaches will call your name from the quaint town of Southport to the ultra-dog-friendly Oak Island. And if you can guess how Sunset Beach got it's name, you'll know why it's worth a visit at the end of the day.

Pack up that doggy sunscreen and throw a towel in your bag because it's time to head to the coast.

The Cape Fear Region

Carolina Beach

Accommodations—Hotels/Motels

Drifters Reef Motel
910-458-5414
701 N. Lake Park Blvd, Carolina Beach, NC 28428

Dog Parks

Mike Chappell Park
Dow Road
Free

 **FUN STUFF!**

Dog-Friendly Beaches

On the north end of Carolina Beach, you and your dog will discover Freeman Park where dogs rule the surf!

From October 1st through March 31st, it's off-leash fun all they way. You must have a 4-wheel-drive vehicle to access the park and both day passes and annual passes are available.

For information, visit www.carolinabeach.org.

Kure Beach

Dog Parks

Gurney Hood Barking Lot
K Avenue at 7th Street
Free

 **FUN STUFF!**

North Carolina Ferry System

All the ferries on the North Carolina Ferry System are dog-friendly and who doesn't love a good boat ride? Leashed dogs are allowed on all outside areas of each ferry.

For a quick trip, the Fort Fisher-Southport Ferry is a fun little 30 minute ride. If you're up for a multi-day trip, try the Cedar Island-Ocracoke Ferry, which has a crossing time of over two hours.

Visit www.ncdot.gov or call 1-800-BY-FERRY for routes and schedule information.

Southport

Accommodations—Hotels/Motels

Comfort Suites
910-454-7444
4963 Southport-Supply Rd, Southport, NC 28461

 FUN STUFF!

Bald Head Island
Great for a day trip or an extended stay, Bald Head Island is just off the coast of Brunswick County. No cars are allowed on the island and it is accessible by private ferry or boat. Renting a golf cart is a fun way to explore Bald Head. North Carolina's oldest standing lighthouse, Old Baldy, is located on the island. Visitors may climb to the top for a $3 donation, but you dog will have to settle for sniffing around the outside.

www.baldheadisland.com

Wilmington

Accommodations—Bed & Breakfasts

Camellia Cottage Bed & Breakfast
866-728-5272
118 South 4th St, Wilmington, NC 28401
www.camelliacottage.net

Accommodations—Hotels/Motels

Baymont Inn & Suites
910-392-67667
306 South College Rd, Wilmington, NC 28403

Days Inn Wilmington Market Street
910-799-6300
5040 Market St, Wilmington, NC 28405

Residence Inn by Marriott Landfall
910-256-0098
1200 Culbreth Dr, Wilmington, NC 28405

🐾 FUN STUFF!

Hook, Line and Paddle
For dogs that have their sea legs, kayaking the intracoastal is a treat in almost any season. Hook, Line and Paddle offers rentals and tours.

877-91-KAYAK/www.hooklineandpaddle.com

Dog Parks

Dog Park at Empie
Park Ave
Free

Ogden Dog Park
Free

 # FUN STUFF!

Masonboro Water Taxi
Don't have a boat but want to enjoy the barrier island of Masonboro?
You and your dog can take the Masonboro Water Taxi. Group tours
are also available.

www.masonborowatertaxi.com
910-540-2260

Trails to Sniff Out

The Loop, Wrightsville Beach
This popular walking trail is a paved sidewalk and can get extremely
crowded during the summer. At one turn in the loop you'll find the
little oasis of Harbor Way Gardens, where you can stop and enjoy some
shade on a bench.

Getting There: *Cross the drawbridge into Wrightsville Beach and
parking is available at Wrightsville Beach Park.*

Oakdale Cemetery, Wilmington
It may not be the first place you think of when considering trails with
your dog, but this historic cemetery is a great spot for you and Fido.
With gravestones dating back to the 1850's, make sure you check out a
tribute to "Boss," the dog who lost his life in a fire in 1880.

Getting There: *Located in historic downtown Wilmington, from
Market Street heading south, turn right onto 15th Street. The
cemetery is at the end of the street.*

TRAIL TIP: Don't let your dog wander off the trail. He could dam-
age plant life or possibly disturb wildlife. It's okay to let him step
off briefly to relieve himself, but make sure you pick up after him.

Hugh MacRae Park, Wilmington

A paved trail runs the perimeter of the park and one of the neat features of this park is that there is an unfenced, off-leash area. Just look for the red posts across from the pond near the south end of the park.

Getting There: *Take College Road South and cross Oleander Drive. The park entrance is on the left at the first stoplight.*

The Riverwalk, Wilmington

Downtown Wilmington is full of sights and sounds and a stroll along the river is perfect any time of the day. The trail runs between Nun Street and Red Cross Street along the Cape Fear River. Wander off the trail for a bit to explore the downtown shops and the residential historic district.

Getting There: *The Riverwalk is located in downtown Wilmington.*

Southport Walking Tour, Southport

You'll love the quaint downtown area of Southport. The historic riverwalk is a beautiful place to start. Pick up a map for a self-guided walking tour of the entire downtown area at the Visitors Center at 113 West Moore Street.

Getting There: *From Hwy 133, take a left on Howe Street and head straight downtown. Take a right on West Moore Street and the Visitors Center is on your left. From NC 211, the highway turns into Howe Street.*

The Crystal Coast

Atlantic Beach

Accommodations—Hotels/Motels

Atlantis Lodge
800-682-7057
123 Salter Path Rd, Atlantic Beach, NC 28512
www.atlantislodge.com

Ramada Inn
252-247-4155
511 Salter Path Rd, Atlantic Beach, NC 28512

Jacksonville

Accommodations—Hotels/Motels

Extended Stay America
910-347-7684
20 McDaniel Dr, Jacksonville, NC 28541

Morehead City

Accommodations—Hotels/Motels

Holiday Inn Express Hotel & Suites
252-247-5001
5063 Executive Dr, Morehead City, NC 28557

 FUN STUFF!

Beaufort Historic Site
As with most places, dogs are not allowed in the buildings, but are welcome on the grounds as long as they are well-behaved and on a leash.

Glimpse a day in the life of a resident of this seaside village from the 18th and 19th centuries. Check out the Old Burying Ground where you'll find graves of revolutionary war soldiers and the oldest legible grave is marked 1756.

The site is located at the 100 block of Turner Street in Beaufort.

www.beauforthistoricsite.org

New Bern

Accommodations—Hotels/Motels

Broad Creek Guest Quarters Resort
252-474-5329
6229 Harbourside Dr, New Bern, NC 28560
www.broadcreekguestquarters.com

Sheraton New Bern Hotel and Marina
800-325-3585
100 Middle St, New Bern, NC 28560

Dog Parks

Downeast Dog Park (at Glenburnie Park)
340 Glenburnie Drive
$35/year - $10/month - $5/day

 FUN STUFF!

Barnacle Bob's
Offering boat and jet ski rentals, they welcome your dog aboard! New Bern is a top boating destination, so if you didn't come by boat, why not rent one for a day on the water? Make sure you call ahead for reservations and let them know your first mate may have four legs.

New Bern Sheraton Marina, Dock F
252-634-4100
www.boatandjetskinewbern.com

Trails to Sniff Out

Neuse River Recreation Area, New Bern

The Neuse River Recreation Area is perfect in the late fall through early spring. If you visit at any other time, make sure you take plenty of bug spray as the mosquitos can be quite nasty.

Getting There: *From New Bern, take US 70 East to NC 1107. Follow signs to the Neuse River Recreation Area.*

Goose Creek State Park, Washington

Eight miles of trails take you through Goose Creek State Park. The namesake Goose Creek Trail is nearly two miles and will take you to the Pamlico river as you discover black gum and cypress swamps. You'll walk under a canopy of live oaks on the Live Oak Trail, a loop that will pass by a cemetery dating from the 1880's. And the Palmetto Boardwalk Trail is an easy jaunt along a boardwalk over a freshwater marsh.

Getting There: *From US 264 turn south on Camp Leach Road. Travel 2.3 miles to the park entrance.*

TRAIL TIP: Never set out on a hike of more than 30 minutes without a water bottle for both you and your dog. Remember, dogs can't tell you when they're thirsty!

Fort Macon State Park, Atlantic Beach

Your pooch will have to sit out if you take a trip inside the fort, but along the shore is the sweet spot for canine play. Hike over the dunes for some fun in the sand at low tide.

Getting There: *Head into Atlantic Beach and the parking lot is located at the end of Route 58.*

Cedar Point Recreation Area, Cedar Point

This is the southwestern corner of the Croatan National Forest in Carteret County. The Tideland Trail is a 1.4 mile loop that is easy to follow. You'll find a mixture of hard sand and boardwalks beneath your feet.

Getting There: *The trailhead is located near the Cedar Point boat ramp parking area. Follow the signs on NC Hwy 58, north of the Hwy 24 junction.*

The Outer Banks

Buxton

Accommodations—Hotels/Motels

Cape Pines Motel
252-995-5666
47497 NC Hwy 12, Buxton, NC 27920

Frisco

Campgrounds

Frisco Campground
53415 Billy Mitchell Rd, Frisco, NC 27936
www.nps.gov

Kill Devil Hills

Accommodations—Hotels/Motels

Quality Inn John Yancey
252-441-7141
2009 South Virginia Dare Trail, Kill Devil Hills, NC 27948

Ramada Plaza Nags Head Beach
252-441-2151
1701 South Virginia Dare Trail, Kill Devil Hills, NC 27948

Travelodge Outer Banks
252-441-0411
804 North Virginia Dare Trail, Kill Devil Hills, NC 27948

Nags Head

Accommodations—Hotels/Motels

Comfort Inn South Oceanfront
252-441-6315
8031 Old Oregon Inlet Rd, Nags Head, NC 27959

Fin & Feather Waterside Inn
888-441-5353
7740 South Virginia Dare Trail, Nags Head, NC 27959
www.finfeatherwatersideinn.com

Ocracoke

Accommodations—Hotels/Motels

Blackbeard's Lodge
800-892-5314
111 Back Rd, Ocracoke, NC 27960
www.blackbeardslodge.com

🐾 FUN STUFF!

Ocracoke Island
A true island getaway, this little gem on the Outer Banks is perfect in any season. There's plenty of walking to be done around the island and all sorts of unique places to explore. Stroll past the Ocracoke Lighthouse built in 1823 and then head to the other side of the island to visit the British Cemetery. You might just stumble upon one of Blackbeard's hiding places!

There is a free ferry that runs from Hatteras (crossing time 40 minutes) and toll ferries from Cedar Island (crossing time 2 hours, 15 minutes) and Swan Quarter (crossing time 2 hours, 45 minutes).

www.ocracokevillage.com

Trails to Sniff Out

Wright Brothers National Memorial, Kill Devil Hills

Head up to Big Kill Devil Hill, the site of those famous glider tests. Stick to the rubber mats, though, as sand spurs will turn this walk into a nightmare.

Getting There: *Take Route 158 to milepost 7.5.*

Jockeys Ridge State Park, Nags Head

Check out the tallest active sand dune system in the Eastern United States at Jockeys Ridge State Park. There's a 1.5 mile walk that takes you over the dunes and to the soundside as well as a one-mile loop along the water.

Getting There: *Located in Nags Head at milepost 12 on the Hwy 158 bypass.*

Buxton Woods Coastal Reserve, Buxton

Nearly 1,000 acres on Hatteras Island are dedicated to this reserve. A number of walking trails connect this state property with the Cape Hatteras National Seashore. This maritime forest is full of pine and live oak. Be careful if visiting between September and February, as the reserve is also part of the NC Game Lands program, and is open to hunters during that time.

Getting There: *The reserve is off of NC 12 and can be accessed via Old Doctor's Road, Flowers Ridge Road or Water Association Road.*

Fort Raleigh National Historic Site, Manteo

This is where the drama of The Lost Colony unfolds and the site of the first English settlement in the New World from 1584 to 1590. There's a short nature trail and a longer hiking trail to the island's western edge.

Getting There: *Take 64 East and the park is located on Roanoke Island, 3 miles north of Manteo.*

TRAIL TIP: Do you have a doggy first aid kit? If not, it's a good idea to have one on hand for hiking excursions. There are plenty of pre-made versions you can buy, or, if you make your own, be sure to include: Scissors, rectal thermometer, hydrogen peroxide, antibiotic ointment, bandages and tape.

State Parks

Carolina Beach State Park
1010 State Park Rd
Carolina Beach, NC 28428
(910) 458-8206

Cliffs of the Neuse State Park
345-A Park Entrance Rd
Seven Springs, NC 28578
(919) 778-6234

Dismal Swamp State Park
2294 US 17 North
South Mills, NC 27976
(252) 771-6593

Fort Fisher State Recreation Area
1000 Loggerhead Rd
Kure Beach, NC 28449
(910) 458-5798

Fort Macon State Park
2300 East Fort Macon Rd
Atlantic Beach, NC, 28512
(252) 726-3775

Goose Creek State Park
2190 Camp Leach Rd
Washington, NC 27889
(252) 923-2191

Hammocks Beach State Park
1572 Hammocks Beach Rd
Swansboro, NC 28584
(910) 326-4881

Jockey's Ridge State Park
Address
Nags Head, NC 27959
(252) 441-7132

Jones Lake State Park
4117 Hwy 242 N
Elizabethtown, NC 28337
(910) 588-4550

Lake Waccamaw State Park
1866 State Park Dr
Lake Waccamaw, NC 28450
(910) 646-4748

Lumber River State Park
2819 Princess Ann Rd
Orrum, NC 28369
(910) 628-4564

Merchants Millpond State Park
71 US Hwy 158E
Gatesville, NC 27938-9440
(252) 357-1191

Pettigrew State Park
2252 Lake Shore Rd
Creswell, NC 27928
(252) 797-4475

Singletary Lake State Park
6707 NC 53 Hwy East
Kelly, NC 28448
(910) 669-2928

Off Leash Dog Parks (by city)

Carolina Beach
Mike Chappell Park
Dow Road
Free

Kure Beach
Gurney Hood Barking Lot
K Avenue at 7th Street
Free

New Bern
Downeast Dog Park (at Glenburnie Park)
340 Glenburnie Drive
$35/year - $10/month - $5/day

Wilmington
Dog Park at Empie
Park Avenue
Free

Ogden Park
Free

Events

FEBRUARY	**Monty's Home Pet Expo,** Wilmington www.montyshome.org
MARCH	**Walk for Those Who Can't,** Wilmington www.walkforthosewhocant.org
MAY	**Paw Jam,** Wilmington www.pawjam.org
SEPTEMBER	**Strutt Your Mutt,** Southport www.barknc.org
OCTOBER	**DogFest,** Wilmington www.cfgoldenrescue.com **Salty Paws Festival,** Carolina Beach

Emergency Vets

WILMINGTON

Animal Emergency Clinic
5333 Oleander Dr
Wilmington, NC 28403
Phone: 910-791-7387

JACKSONVILLE

Coastal Veterinary Emergency
1200 Hargett St
Jacksonville, NC 28540
Phone: 910-455-3838

Index

Index

Index

About the Author

Suzanne Jalot is a freelance writer and is the founder and editor of Dog Living Magazine, a bimonthly publication for dog lovers in North Carolina. Suzanne has been a North Carolina resident since she was eight, so she's had plenty of time to explore this great state. She loves nothing more than traveling with her two large mutts, Ollie and August, and loves finding new spots that both she and her dogs can enjoy. She lives in Wilmington, North Carolina with her dogs, a bi-polar cat, and one very understanding spouse.

Know of places we missed? Make sure we include them in the next edition! Email editor@doglivingmagazine.com.

COUPONS

WAG: RALEIGH'S PREMIER PET BOUTIQUE

- Best in food, treats & accessories
- On-site specialists to help with all your needs.

919-841-5093
www.wagpets.com

20% OFF

ALL NON-FOOD MERCHANDISE

Bring this coupon to the store
to redeem. Offer valid through 12/31/2010.

Stonehenge Market • 7414 Creedmoor Road • Raleigh, NC

Pet Loss Grief Support & Canine Rescue

Visit us online to learn more about our
Pet Expo, held in February, and our
Pawsitive Partners Prison Program!!

www.montyshome.org